Sweet and Savory Tarts

Tarts

The Most Delicious Sweet and Savory Tart Recipes Ever!

BY: Valeria Ray

License Notes

Table of Contents

Introduction

Whether you're gearing up for a bake sale or simply want to treat yourself or your loved ones to something sweet or savory, you need to look no further than this recipe book. You'll find 30 of the most mouth-watering tart recipes here.

Ranging from traditional flavors like lemon tart and apple tart to flavors like caramelized onion and feta tart, this recipe book has it all. Each recipe in this book has detailed, step-by-step instructions that will guarantee the most delicious tarts you have ever eaten. So what are you waiting for? Choose a recipe, grab your tart pan, and let's get baking!

1. Lemon Tart

Sweet, zesty and light, this tart is the perfect after-dessert treat.

Makes: 8 servings

Prep: 2 hrs. 10 mins

Cook: 30 mins

Ingredients:

For the pastry:

- 1 ¾ cup all-purpose flour
- 4 tbsp. icing sugar
- ½ tsp salt
- ¼ cup unsweetened cocoa powder
- ½ cup unsalted butter
- 1 egg yolk
- 2 ½ tbsp. cold water

For the tart:

- ½ cup dark chocolate, grated finely
- 2 large lemons
- 2/3 cup caster sugar
- 4 eggs
- ½ cup + 2 tbsp. heavy cream
- Icing sugar, for dusting

Directions:

For the pastry:

In a bowl, combine together the salt, cocoa, sugar, and flour. Add the butter and mix. Add the egg yolk and then the water. Mix well. Fold into a lump. Wrap with cling film and chill for 40 minutes.

Roll out the pastry evenly onto the base of a well-greased 9-inch spring form cake tin and chill for 90 minutes.

For the tart:

Preheat oven to 400°F. Place in the oven for 15 minutes. Do not overbake. Immediately sprinkle the hot pastry evenly with the grated chocolate. Set aside. Reduce oven temperature to 325°F.

Grate the zest into a bowl. Add the sugar and the juice from the lemons. Mix well. Whisk in the eggs and then the cream until well incorporated. Pour over the pastry in the spring form tin and bake for about 30 minutes or until set.

Release the spring form-tin sides to aid cooling. Allow to cool completely. Dust with sugar and serve.

2. White Chocolate Raspberry Tart

Raspberry and white chocolate tart with a chocolate shortbread pastry crust.

Makes: 4 servings

Prep: 20 mins

Cook: 20 mins

Ingredients:

For the chocolate shortbread pastry:

- 1 ¼ cups all-purpose flour
- 3/8 cup unsalted butter
- Generous 3/8 cup white sugar
- 2 egg yolks
- 1/4 tsp baking powder
- 7 tsp cocoa powder
- Vanilla powder
- Salt

For the filling:

- Generous 3/8 cup cream
- 2 tsp glucose syrup
- 7 oz. white chocolate
- 3 oz. raspberry jam

For the decoration:

- 9 oz. fresh raspberries
- Confectioners' (icing) sugar

Directions:

Prepare the shortbread pastry: Mix the softened butter with the sugar, stir in a pinch of salt and the egg. Add the flour, baking powder, cocoa and a pinch of vanilla powder, then knead briefly until you have a smooth, even paste.

Plastic wrap the dough and refrigerate for one hour. On a lightly floured surface, roll out 9 oz. of the shortbread pastry to a thickness of 1/8 in (3 mm).

Line a buttered, floured cake tin with the pastry. Spread with raspberry jam and bake at 350 °F (180 °C) for 18 to 20 minutes. Remove and cool, then remove the tart from the tin.

Chop the white chocolate and put it in a bowl. Boil the cream with the syrup and pour it over the chocolate. Mix well until you have smooth, velvety cream.

Leave to cool and pour into the tart shell until it is filled up to the brim. Garnish with fresh raspberries, which have been washed and dried. Sprinkle with confectioners' sugar before serving.

3. Wild Mushroom- And Caramelized Red Onion Tarte Tatin

If you are unable to get wild mushrooms, this tart works fine with a mix of cremini, button, and Portobello mushrooms. This is a great appetizer recipe.

Makes: 6 servings

Prep: 1 hr. 20 mins

Cook: 30 mins

Ingredients:

Pie Crust

- 1½ cups all-purpose flour
- ½ teaspoon salt
- 6 tbsp. cold unsalted butter, cut into cubes
- 2 tablespoons cold shortening
- 5 to 6 tablespoons ice water

Filling

- 2 tablespoons olive oil, divided
- 2 tablespoons butter, divided
- ½ red onion, root end trimmed, peeled and cut into 6 to 8 (½-inch) wedges
- 1 teaspoon sugar
- ½ shallot, peeled and minced
- 8 cups assorted wild mushrooms, sliced
- 1 teaspoon fresh thyme
- ¼ teaspoon salt
- Freshly ground black pepper
- 2 tablespoons Madeira, sherry, or balsamic vinegar
- ¼ cup heavy cream
- 1 teaspoon fresh thyme, for garnish

- ¼ cup crumbled blue cheese, for garnish

Directions:

To prepare the pastry dough, in a large bowl, mix together the flour and salt. With a pastry knife or your fingers, add the butter and the shortening, working quickly to blend with the flour until the mixture resembles small peas. Do not overwork. Add 1 to 2 tablespoons ice water at a time and mix well, using your hands. Once you have added all of the water, form the dough into a ball or flat disk. Wrap and refrigerate for at 1 hour. (Alternately, you can prepare the dough in a food processor: add the flour and salt, pulse once, and then add half of the butter and the shortening and pulse twice. Add the rest of the butter and shortening and pulse five times, or until the mixture resembles small peas. Add the water 1-2 tbsp at a time, pulsing once or twice between each addition. Once you have added all of the water, form the dough into a ball or disk, wrap, & refrigerate for at least 1 hr.)

To prepare the filling, place a rack in the upper third of the oven and preheat to 400°F.

In a 10- or 12-inch cast iron skillet over medium heat, warm 1 tablespoon each of the olive oil and butter. Add the onion wedges and cook for 5 minutes. Flip the onions, sprinkle with the sugar, and cook for 5 minutes longer. Remove to a plate.

Add the remaining tbsp each of olive oil and butter to the pan. Add the shallots and cook for 2 mins. Add the mushrooms and cook for 10-15 mins, stirring occasionally. After the mushrooms have released their moisture and begun to brown, add the thyme, salt, and pepper. Cook until they start to turn brown. Add the Madeira and cook for 1 minute. Add the cream and cook for 2 minutes. Add the onion wedges back to the pan with the mushrooms. Remove & set aside.

On a slightly floured surface, roll dough into a circle. Place the dough on top, tucking it in if needed. Make three slits in the top to vent the tart while cooking. Place it on the upper rack and bake for 15 minutes, or until the tart is golden. Remove the skillet from the oven. Place a plate that is slightly bigger than the skillet atop the skillet. Using two pot holders, grasp the skillet and plate tightly, quickly flip the skillet, and wait for about 5 seconds before carefully setting the plate on the counter and removing the skillet. If some filling remains in the skillet, place it back on the tart. Sprinkle with salt, garnish with thyme and blue cheese, and serve.

4. Tarte Tatin

A classic French dessert, tarte Tatin was meant to be cooked in a cast iron skillet. The apples caramelize perfectly and make a beautiful presentation when the tart is inverted.

Makes: 8 servings

Prep: 1 hr.

Cook: 30 mins

Ingredients:

Pastry

- 1 cup all-purpose flour
- ½ teaspoon salt
- 1 tablespoon sugar
- 6 tbsp unsalted butter, cubed
- 3 tablespoons ice-cold water

Filling

- 1 cup unsalted butter, cubed
- 1½ cups sugar
- 8 to 9 apples (Jonagold, Fuji, or Golden Delicious), peeled, cored, and halved

Directions:

Combine the flour, salt, and sugar into a medium bowl. Rub the butter into the flour mixture with your fingers until it resembles coarse crumbs. Sprinkle the water into the mixture, and gently work it into the dough just until the dough holds together. Form into a ball, wrap , & refrigerate for 30 minutes or overnight.

To prepare the filling, scatter the butter pieces evenly over the bottom of a 10-inch cast iron skillet. Sprinkle the sugar evenly over the butter, covering the pan bottom. Arrange the apples tightly together in the skillet in a circular pattern, starting at the outside and working toward the center. The apple halves should be on their sides, holding each other up and all facing the same direction. Place 2 halves in the center of the pan. (During cooking, the apples will slide down more into the pan.)

Place the skillet over med-low heat and cook, uncovered, until the sugar begins to caramelize (turn golden brown), 35 to 40 minutes. During cooking, spoon some of the caramelized juices over the apples to help caramelize them.

Preheat to 400°F.

Remove dough & roll out on a slightly floured surface into a 12-inch circle. Drape the pastry dough over the apples, tucking the excess dough into the skillet without disturbing the apples. Put the skillet on a baking pan in the oven, and bake until the pastry is golden brown, 20 to 25 minutes.

Remove & let the tart sit for 3 minutes. Find a plate that is slightly larger than the skillet. Turn it upside down on top of the skillet. Protecting both hands with oven mitts, grasp the cast iron skillet and the plate firmly with both hands, pressing the plate tightly onto the skillet. Invert the tart onto the plate. Serve.

5. Plum Galette

A galette is a free-form tart. You roll out the pastry and then fold the edges over the fruit. Served in the cast iron skillet, this rustic dessert, with its golden crust and shiny, glazed plums, makes a beautiful presentation at the table.

Makes: 6 servings

Prep: 1 hr.

Cook: 30 mins

Ingredients:

Pastry

- ⅓ cup sour cream
- ½ cup ice-cold water
- 1½ cups all-purpose flour
- ⅓ cup yellow cornmeal
- 3 teaspoons sugar, plus 1 tablespoon for sprinkling on the prebaked dough
- ½ teaspoon salt
- 10 tablespoons chilled unsalted butter, cut into 8 pieces

Filling

- 20 Italian plums, halved and pitted, or 10 of the larger variety plums, quartered
- ½ cup sugar
- 2 tablespoons cornstarch
- 2 teaspoons fresh lemon juice

Glaze

- 5 tablespoons plum jam or marmalade
- 3 tablespoons water

Directions:

To prepare the pastry, whisk together the sour cream and ice water in a small bowl. Set aside.

Place the flour, cornmeal, the 3 teaspoons sugar, and salt in a large bowl. Mix with a dry whisk or your fingers until well blended. Add the butter. Mix with your hands, a pastry blender, or in a food processor until the pieces of butter are pea-sized (8 to 10 pulses in the food processor). Add the sour cream mixture, 1 tablespoon at a time, gently mixing after each addition. Once all the liquid has been added, form the dough into a large disk. Don't handle the dough too much and work quickly so that the butter stays cold. Wrap & refrigerate for 1 to 2 hours.

Place the plums in a large bowl with the sugar, cornstarch, and lemon juice.

Preheat to 400°F.

To prepare the glaze, place the jam, water in a saucepan. Bring to a boil over med-low heat. Remove from the heat and set aside.

To prepare the galette, roll out the chilled dough on a slightly floured surface until you have a 14- to 16-inch circle. Lightly flour the top of the dough. Fold dough over the pin & transfer to an 8-inch cast iron skillet. Gently press into the bottom and against the sides of the skillet. It just needs to stick to the sides while you add the filling. Arrange the plums in the pan in a circular pattern, slightly overlapping one another, skin side up, starting at the outer edges and working toward the center. Quickly reheat the glaze and spoon over the plums. Fold the edges over the fruit. It will form pleats, which is the result you want. You should have a roughly 2- to 3-inch border of dough folded in all around the edges. Sprinkle the plums and crust with the 1 tablespoon sugar. Bake for 25 to 30 minutes. Serve in the skillet with vanilla ice cream or whipped cream.

6. Provençal Onion, Tomato, and Olive Tart

Pissaladières are popular pizza-like snacks in the south of France.

Makes: 4-6 servings

Prep: 1 hr. 10 mins

Cook: 40 mins

Ingredients:

- 1 (14-ounce) package all-butter puff pastry, defrosted
- 3⁄4 pound yellow onions, peeled, cut in half lengthwise and thinly sliced crosswise
- 2 Tablespoons olive oil
- 2 Tablespoons white balsamic vinegar
- 1⁄2 Tablespoon herbes de Provence
- 1⁄2 teaspoon salt
- Freshly ground black pepper
- 3 Tablespoons sugar
- 1 1⁄2 Tablespoons water
- 2 ⁄3 cup (3 ounces) sun-dried tomatoes, blotted dry and thinly sliced
- 1⁄3 cup (2 ounces) pitted oil-cured black olives, chopped

Directions:

Preheat your oven to 425°F. Unfold the pastry and, using a circular pattern, cut it into an 11-inch round; lay the dough on a cutting board, cover with a towel, and refrigerate for hour.

Meanwhile, heat a 10-inch cast-iron skillet over medium-high heat until hot but not smoking, 3 ½ to 4 minutes. In a bowl, combine onions and oil; add them to the skillet and sauté over med-low heat until they are golden, about 15 minutes, stirring often. Pour in the vinegar, raise the heat to high, and boil until the vinegar evaporates, about 30 seconds, stirring often. Scrape the onions into a bowl, then stir in the herbes de Provence, salt, and a generous amount of pepper.

Wipe skillet & heat it over medium-high heat. Add the sugar and water and cook until the sugar melts and turns a rich amber brown, about 5 minutes, rotating the pan to coat it evenly. Remove & spoon the onions over the caramel; scatter the tomatoes and olives evenly over the onions and lay the puff pastry on top, tucking the edges into the pan. With a sharp knife, make four or five 1-inch cuts in the top.

Bake for 10 minutes; adjust the heat down to 350°F & continue baking until the crust is puffed & golden, about 20 mins. Remove and let it stand for 5 mins. Run a knife around the edges of the pan to loosen the pastry, then place a 10-inch plate directly on the pissaladière and flip it out. Replace any ingredients that remain in the pan. With a serrated knife, cut the pissaladière into wedges and serve.

7. Apple-Cherry Tarte Tatin

In this upside-down tart, the thick apple slices are complemented by tangy dried cherries.

Makes: 8 servings

Prep: 1 hr. 10 mins

Cook: 40 mins

Ingredients:

- ¼ cup dried cherries
- 2 Tablespoons apple juice
- 1 (15-ounce) package all-butter puff pastry, defrosted according to package directions
- 5 to 6 medium firm, tart-sweet apples, such as Jonagold, Cortland, Northern Spy, Golden Delicious
- Juice of 1 to 2 lemons
- ¾ cup sugar
- 1 Tablespoon water
- 4 Tablespoons unsalted butter, cut into small pieces
- Crème fraiche or sweetened whipped cream, to garnish

Directions:

In a small bowl, combine the cherries with the juice and set aside. Roll out pastry on a slightly floured surface to a thickness of ⅛ inch. With a sharp knife, cut it into an 11-inch circle and brush off any excess flour. Lay the pastry on a cutting board, cover with a towel, and refrigerate.

Peel and core the apples; slice them in half lengthwise, then cut each half in thirds lengthwise. Put in a bowl & drizzle with lemon juice as you cut them to prevent discoloring.

Preheat your oven to 400°F. Put the sugar in a 10-inch cast-iron skillet and drizzle on the water. Turn the heat to high and cook until the sugar melts into a rich, golden amber-colored syrup, 6 to 7 minutes, swirling and shaking the pan often to melt it evenly. Watch that it doesn't burn. Immediately remove, add the butter (it might bubble up), and stir until it is incorporated. Continue stirring the mixture until the caramel cools, 3 to 4 minutes. If the sugar seizes up when you add the butter, return the pan to the heat to re-melt it.

Lay the apple slices on the caramel around the outside of the pan, on their side and each in the same direction with the stem end closest to the pan's edge. Put the remaining apple slices in the center. (You may not need all of the apples.) Drain the cherries and add them around the edges, between each apple slice, and in the middle.

Remove pastry from the refrigerator and lay it over the apples, pushing the edges down the sides of the pan. Cut 3 or 4 small gashes in the surface of the pastry as air vents, then transfer to the oven & bake for 10 mins. Reduce the heat to 375°F and bake for 20 minutes longer.

Remove and cool the tart for about 20 minutes in the pan. Using a plate with a lip that is slightly larger than the skillet, put it upside down over the skillet and, holding them together with one hand, invert the skillet and let the tart slide out onto the plate, rearranging any apples that may have moved. Using a pie server with a sharp edge, cut the tart into slices and serve.

8. Tomato and Dijon Mustard Tartes Fines

These individual tarts are great for starters or a light meal.

Makes: 6 servings

Prep: 15 mins

Cook: 15 mins

Ingredients:

- 500g (1lb) ready-made or homemade puff pastry
- Plain flour, for dusting
- 1 egg yolk, beaten
- 6 tsp Dijon mustard
- 6 plum tomatoes, sliced lengthways
- Fresh or dried oregano, for sprinkling
- Olive oil
- 6 × 125g (4oz) buffalo mozzarella balls, drained
- Bunch of wild rocket
- Salt and freshly ground black pepper

Directions:

Preheat the oven to 400°F.

Roll out the pastry on a slightly floured surface to 3mm (1/3in) thick. Using a pastry cutter, cut out 6 × 15cm (6in) discs and place them on 2 baking sheets.

Brush the egg yolk around the inside edges of the discs with a pastry brush. Lightly prick the centers with a fork. Spread a good layer of mustard in the center of each disc, keeping the glazed edge clean.

Place the tomatoes overlapping on top of the mustard. Season with salt and pepper and sprinkle with either fresh or dried oregano and a light drizzle of olive oil.

Bake for 15–20 mins.

Place the warm tarts on individual serving plates. Using a knife, cut a deep gash in the top of each mozzarella ball. Place a ball in the center of each tart and stuff with fresh rocket. Drizzle with olive oil and serve.

9. White Chocolate Blueberry Tart

Blueberry and white chocolate tart with a chocolate shortbread pastry crust.

Makes: 4 servings

Prep: 20 mins

Cook: 20 mins

Ingredients:

For the chocolate shortbread pastry:

- 1 ¼ cups all-purpose flour
- 3/8 cup unsalted butter
- Generous 3/8 cup white sugar
- 2 egg yolks
- 1/4 tsp baking powder
- 7 tsp cocoa powder
- Vanilla powder
- Salt

For the filling:

- Generous 3/8 cup cream
- 2 tsp glucose syrup
- 7 oz. white chocolate
- 3 oz. blueberry jam

For the decoration:

- 9 oz. fresh blueberries
- Confectioners' (icing) sugar

Directions:

Prepare the shortbread pastry: Mix the softened butter with the sugar, stir in a pinch of salt and the egg. Add the flour, baking powder, cocoa and a pinch of vanilla powder, then knead briefly until you have a smooth, even paste.

Plastic wrap the dough and refrigerate for one hour. On a lightly floured surface, roll out 9 oz. of the shortbread pastry to a thickness of 1/8 in (3 mm).

Line a buttered, floured cake tin with the pastry. Spread with blueberry jam and bake at 350 °F (180 °C) for 18 to 20 minutes. Remove and cool, then remove the tart from the tin.

Chop the white chocolate and put it in a bowl. Boil the cream with the syrup and pour it over the chocolate. Mix well until you have smooth, velvety cream.

Leave to cool and pour into the tart shell until it is filled up to the brim. Garnish with fresh blueberries, which have been washed and dried. Sprinkle with confectioners' sugar before serving.

10. Orange Tart

Sweet, zesty and light, this is a classic orange tart recipe.

Makes: 8 servings

Prep: 2 hrs. 10 mins

Cook: 30 mins

Ingredients:

For the pastry:

- 1 ¾ cup all-purpose flour
- 4 tbsp. icing sugar
- ½ tsp salt
- ¼ cup unsweetened cocoa powder
- ½ cup unsalted butter
- 1 egg yolk
- 2 ½ tbsp. cold water

For the tart:

- ½ cup dark chocolate, grated finely
- 2 oranges
- 2/3 cup caster sugar
- 4 eggs
- ½ cup + 2 tbsp. heavy cream
- Icing sugar, for dusting

Directions:

For the pastry:

In a bowl, combine together the salt, cocoa, sugar, and flour. Add the butter and mix. Add the egg yolk and then the water. Mix well. Fold into a lump. Wrap with cling film and chill for 40 minutes.

Roll out the pastry evenly onto the base of a well-greased 9-inch spring form cake tin and chill for 90 minutes.

For the tart:

Preheat oven to 400°F. Place in the oven for 15 minutes. Do not overbake. Immediately sprinkle the hot pastry evenly with the grated chocolate. Set aside. Reduce oven temperature to 325°F.

Grate the zest into a bowl. Add the sugar and the juice from the oranges. Mix well. Whisk in the eggs and then the cream until well incorporated. Pour over the pastry in the spring form tin and bake for about 30 minutes or until set.

Release the spring form-tin sides to aid cooling. Allow to cool completely. Dust with sugar and serve.

11. Artichoke and Black Olive Tart

Delicious savory tart with marinated artichokes and olives.

Makes: 8 servings

Prep: 10 mins

Cook: 25 mins

Ingredients:

- 7 oz. marinated artichokes, drained and cut into quarters
- 3 oz. black Kalamata olives, pitted and roughly chopped
- 1 × blind-baked short crust pastry case with 1 oz. grated Parmesan cheese added
- 5oz. soft goats' cheese
- 1/2 cup heavy cream
- 3 eggs
- 1 tbsp fresh thyme leaves
- Salt and freshly ground black pepper

Directions:

Preheat the oven to 350°F

Arrange the both artichokes and black olives in the base of the cooked pastry base.

Mix the goats' cheese with the remaining ingredients, then season with salt and pepper.

Pour the mixture over and bake in the oven for 25 minutes, or until just set and light golden.

12. Black Pudding and Apple Tart

Black pudding with apples and cream.

Makes: 8 servings

Prep: 15 mins

Cook: 40 mins

Ingredients:

- 50g (2oz) unsalted butter
- 250g (8oz) Cox's or Granny Smith apples, peeled, cored and quartered
- 150ml (¼ pint) heavy cream
- 100ml (3½fl oz.) milk
- 2 large eggs
- 2 teaspoon ground allspice
- 250g (8oz) black pudding
- 1 × blind-baked short crust pastry case
- 2 tbsp thyme leaves
- 2 bay leaves
- Salt and freshly ground black pepper

Directions:

Preheat the oven to 350°F

Melt the butter in a pan. Add the apple quarters and fry over a medium heat until they have a nice golden color but are not mushy. Remove apples from the pan and put to one side.

In a bowl, mix the cream with the milk, eggs and allspice, and season with salt and pepper. Cut the black pudding into pieces and place in the cooked pastry base. Place the apple quarters in between the pieces of black pudding.

Sprinkle with the thyme leaves. Break up the bay leaves and arrange on top. Pour in the egg & cream mixture and bake for 30 mins.

13. Baked Raspberry and Basil Tart

Sometimes fresh herbs or spices help to boost the original flavor of ingredients – black pepper with strawberries, salt with chocolate. In this case it's the fresh flavor of basil to enhance the raspberries.

Makes: 8 servings

Prep: 15 mins

Cook: 20 mins

Ingredients:

- 1 × plain sponge cake, 20cm (8in) in diameter
- 1 × blind-baked sweet short crust pastry case
- 5 tbsp raspberry jam
- 500g (1lb) raspberries

For the basil syrup

- 125ml (4fl oz.) water
- 125g (4oz) golden caster sugar
- 6 basil leaves

Directions:

To make the basil syrup, put the water and sugar into a saucepan and heat to boiling point. Add the basil & leave to infuse for as long as possible – ideally overnight.

Preheat the oven to 400F. Cut the sponge cake in half, horizontally across the center.

Spread one 1/2 of the cake with raspberry jam and place it jam side down in the cooked pastry shell. Put the other 1/2 of the sponge cake to one side for another day.

Remove the basil leaves & discard them, then spoon the syrup over the sponge until it is evenly soaked.

Cover the tart with the raspberries and bake in the oven for 15 minutes or until the raspberries are hot and oozing juice. Serve immediately.

14. Chocolate Crumble Tart

A chocolate crumble with baked apple and pear.

Makes: 8 servings

Prep: 20 mins

Cook: 50 mins

Ingredients:

- 2 apples
- 2 pears
- 25g (1oz) unsalted butter
- 1 tbsp dark rum
- 75g (3oz) dark muscovado sugar
- 125g (4oz) unsalted butter, softened
- 125g (4oz) golden caster sugar
- 50g (2oz) cocoa powder
- 125g (4oz) ground almonds
- 3 eggs
- 1 × uncooked chocolate short crust pastry case
- Icing sugar and cocoa powder, for dusting

For the crumble

- 100g (3½oz) plain flour
- 25g (1oz) cocoa powder
- 50g (2oz) light muscovado sugar
- 50g (2oz) unsalted butter

Directions:

Preheat the oven to 325°F.

Peel & core the apples & pears and chop them into cubes.
Melt the butter & add the fruit, rum and dark muscovado
sugar. Cook over a med. heat until the fruit has colored but
is not mushy. Put to one side.

In a bowl beat the butter, caster sugar, cocoa powder and
ground almonds. Beat in the 3 eggs, 1 at a time. Using a
spatula, spread the chocolate and almond cream in the
uncooked pastry case until half full. Top with the cooked
apple and pear.

To make the crumble, rub together all the crumble
ingredients with your fingertips. Generously spread this
over the tart.

Bake for 45–50 mins, or until golden.

15. Treacle Tart

A delicious tart made with golden syrup, breadcrumbs and lemons.

Makes: 12 servings

Prep: 30 mins

Cook: 40 mins

Ingredients:

For the pastry case:

- 2 ½ cups all-purpose flour
- 1 tsp salt
- 2 tbsp sugar
- 2 ½ sticks (280g/10oz) butter
- 5-6 tbsp cold water

For the filling:

- 1 cup golden syrup
- 2 ½ cups fresh breadcrumbs (made from crust less toasted bread)
- 1 lemon
- 1 egg + 1 tbsp water for brushing the pastry
- Clotted cream or double cream, for serving

Directions:

For the pastry: Cut butter into 1 inch cubes, layer them on a tray and freeze for about 15 mins. They should be really cold but not frozen.

Meanwhile, in a food processor, add ⅔ of the flour, sugar and salt and mix well.

Add the chilled butter cubes and process shortly, until the dough just begins to clump. Sprinkle the remaining flour and pulse for about 10 more seconds.

Transfer the mixture to a bowl. Sprinkle 5 tablespoons of the cold water and fold it in using a spatula until the dough comes together. Only add more water if the dough doesn't hold together between your fingers.

Form a ball out of the dough and divide it into two discs, one slightly larger than the other. Refrigerate for 2 hours or overnight.

Preheat oven to 400°F. On a floured surface, roll the bigger disc of dough until it covers the bottom and the edges of the pie pan. Carefully place the rolled dough into your pan, pressing the pastry into the edges of the pan.

Roll out the second dough into a 9-inch circle of around 1/8 inch thickness. Cut out long strips for the lattice topping.

For the filling: Start by making your breadcrumbs. Cut out the crusts of the toasted bread, weigh out 110g of bread needed and process in a food processor. Next, juice and zest the lemon.

In a saucepan, heat the syrup until runny. Remove from heat and add in the breadcrumbs, zest and juice. Put the filling into the pan and using a spatula, even out the top.

Lay half of the dough strips over the filling in one direction and the other half in the other direction to form the lattice. Trim the edges.

Brush the edges and the lattice with the egg and water mixture. Bake for 10 mins at 400°F, then reduce heat to 375°F and bake for 25 minutes more or until the crust turns golden-brown and the filling is just set.

Serve with clotted or thick cream.

16. White Chocolate Strawberry Tart

Strawberry and white chocolate tart with a chocolate shortbread pastry crust.

Makes: 4 servings

Prep: 20 mins

Cook: 20 mins

Ingredients:

For the chocolate shortbread pastry:

- 1 ¼ cups all-purpose flour
- 3/8 cup unsalted butter
- Generous 3/8 cup white sugar
- 2 egg yolks
- 1/4 tsp baking powder
- 7 tsp cocoa powder
- Vanilla powder
- Salt

For the filling:

- Generous 3/8 cup cream
- 2 tsp glucose syrup
- 7 oz. white chocolate
- 3 oz. strawberry jam

For the decoration:

- 9 oz. fresh strawberries
- Confectioners' (icing) sugar

Directions:

Prepare the shortbread pastry: Mix the softened butter with the sugar, stir in a pinch of salt and the egg. Add the flour, baking powder, cocoa and a pinch of vanilla powder, then knead briefly until you have a smooth, even paste.

Plastic wrap the dough and refrigerate for one hour. On a lightly floured surface, roll out 9 oz. of the shortbread pastry to a thickness of 1/8 in (3 mm).

Line a buttered, floured cake tin with the pastry. Spread with strawberry jam and bake at 350 °F (180 °C) for 18 to 20 minutes. Remove and cool, then remove the tart from the tin.

Chop the white chocolate and put it in a bowl. Boil the cream with the syrup and pour it over the chocolate. Mix well until you have smooth, velvety cream.

Leave to cool and pour into the tart shell until it is filled up to the brim. Garnish with fresh strawberries, which have been washed and dried. Sprinkle with confectioners' sugar before serving.

17. Apple and Almond Nougat Tart

The combination of the nuts and the sweet honey taste of the nougat works very well with the chunky apple slices.

Makes: 8 servings

Prep: 15 mins

Cook: 30 mins

Ingredients:

Preparation time: 15 minutes

Cooking time: 30 minutes

- 2 eggs
- 50g (2oz) golden caster sugar
- 1 tbsp corn flour
- 150ml (¼ pint) milk
- 1 tbsp double cream
- 100g (3½oz) nougat
- 3 apples (Granny Smith or Cox's), peeled, cored and chopped into chunky slices
- 1 × blind-baked sweet short crust pastry case
- 50g (2oz) golden sultanas
- 25g (1oz) shelled pistachio nuts, chopped

Directions:

Preheat the oven to 325°F

Put the eggs & sugar into a bowl and cream together until pale and creamy. Beat in the corn flour.

Put the milk, cream and nougat into a saucepan and bring to the boil. Stir until the nougat has melted. Pour over the egg mix & mix well with a whisk.

Arrange the apple slices in the cooked pastry case and scatter over the sultanas and pistachio nuts. Pour the nougat custard over the apples and bake in the oven for 30–35 minutes, or until set and golden.

18. Chocolate Raspberry Tart

Raspberry and chocolate tart with a chocolate shortbread pastry crust.

Makes: 4 servings

Prep: 20 mins

Cook: 20 mins

Ingredients:

For the chocolate shortbread pastry:

- 1 ¼ cups all-purpose flour
- 3/8 cup unsalted butter
- Generous 3/8 cup white sugar
- 2 egg yolks
- 1/4 tsp baking powder
- 7 tsp cocoa powder
- Vanilla powder
- Salt

For the filling:

- Generous 3/8 cup cream
- 2 tsp glucose syrup
- 7 oz. dark chocolate
- 3 oz. raspberry jam

For the decoration:

- 9 oz. fresh raspberries
- Confectioners' (icing) sugar

Directions:

Prepare the shortbread pastry: Mix the softened butter with the sugar, stir in a pinch of salt and the egg. Add the flour, baking powder, cocoa and a pinch of vanilla powder, then knead briefly until you have a smooth, even paste.

Plastic wrap the dough and refrigerate for one hour. On a lightly floured surface, roll out 9 oz. of the shortbread pastry to a thickness of 1/8 in (3 mm).

Line a buttered, floured cake tin with the pastry. Spread with raspberry jam and bake at 350 °F (180 °C) for 18 to 20 minutes. Remove and cool, then remove the tart from the tin.

Chop the chocolate and put it in a bowl. Boil the cream with the syrup and pour it over the chocolate. Mix well until you have smooth, velvety cream.

Leave to cool and pour into the tart shell until it is filled up to the brim. Garnish with fresh raspberries, which have been washed and dried. Sprinkle with confectioners' sugar before serving.

19. Chocolate Blueberry Tart

Blueberry and chocolate tart with a chocolate shortbread pastry crust.

Makes: 4 servings

Prep: 20 mins

Cook: 20 mins

Ingredients:

For the chocolate shortbread pastry:

- 1 ¼ cups all-purpose flour
- 3/8 cup unsalted butter
- Generous 3/8 cup white sugar
- 2 egg yolks
- 1/4 tsp baking powder
- 7 tsp cocoa powder
- Vanilla powder
- Salt

For the filling:

- Generous 3/8 cup cream
- 2 tsp glucose syrup
- 7 oz. dark chocolate
- 3 oz. blueberry jam

For the decoration:

- 9 oz. fresh blueberries
- Confectioners' (icing) sugar

Directions:

Prepare the shortbread pastry: Mix the softened butter with the sugar, stir in a pinch of salt and the egg. Add the flour, baking powder, cocoa and a pinch of vanilla powder, then knead briefly until you have a smooth, even paste.

Plastic wrap the dough and refrigerate for one hour. On a lightly floured surface, roll out 9 oz. of the shortbread pastry to a thickness of 1/8 in (3 mm).

Line a buttered, floured cake tin with the pastry. Spread with blueberry jam and bake at 350 °F (180 °C) for 18 to 20 minutes. Remove and cool, then remove the tart from the tin.

Chop the chocolate and put it in a bowl. Boil the cream with the syrup and pour it over the chocolate. Mix well until you have smooth, velvety cream.

Leave to cool and pour into the tart shell until it is filled up to the brim. Garnish with fresh blueberries, which have been washed and dried. Sprinkle with confectioners' sugar before serving.

20. Curried Chicken Tart

This is a very flavorsome tart and you can make it as spicy as you want, but I like mine mild. A salad of leaves and lots of fresh coriander is the perfect accompaniment.

Makes: 8 servings

Prep: 15 mins

Cook: 50 mins

Ingredients:

- 375g (12oz) ready-made or homemade puff pastry
- Plain flour, for dusting
- 2 tbsp vegetable oil
- 1 onion, thinly sliced
- 400g (13oz) chicken breast fillets, cut into strips
- 4 tbsp Thai red curry paste
- 400ml (14fl oz.) coconut cream
- 1 tomato, peeled, deseeded and chopped
- 200g (7oz) canned or fresh pineapple, chopped
- 2 eggs
- Bunch of fresh coriander, roughly chopped
- Salt and freshly ground black pepper

Directions:

Preheat the oven to 350F.

Roll out the pastry on a slightly floured surface to 3–4mm (1/5in) thick and use it to line a 23cm (9in) diameter, 4.5cm (1¾in) deep tart tin. Blind bake (see blind baking).

Heat the veg. oil in a frying pan, and then add the onion and fry until it has browned and softened. Add the chicken & stir-fry for 2–3 mins. Stir in the curry paste, half the coconut cream, the tomato and the pineapple pieces. Simmer for 10–12 mins, stirring occasionally, until the sauce has greatly reduced and thickened. Allow to cool for 5 minutes.

Blend the eggs in a bowl with the rest of the coconut cream and add the coriander. Stir into the curry mixture, then season with salt and pepper.

Fill the cooked pastry base with the mixture and bake in the oven for 30 minutes, or until set and golden.

Serve warm, alongside a fresh coriander salad dressed with sesame oil and finely chopped shallots.

21. Caramelized Onion and Feta Tarts

These little individual tarts are perfect as a light starter or to take on a picnic or outdoor meal. The long, slow cooking of the red onion gives a lovely sweet taste that is enhanced by the balsamic vinegar. The feta cheese and the part-baked tomatoes cut through the sweetness wonderfully.

Makes: 6 servings

Prep: 20 mins

Cook: 1 hr.

Ingredients:

- 200g (7oz) cherry tomatoes, cut in half
- 3 tbsp extra virgin olive oil
- 1 garlic clove, finely chopped
- 25g (1oz) unsalted butter
- 625g (1¼lb) red onions, thinly sliced
- 2 tbsp balsamic vinegar
- 6 × blind-baked puff pastry cases, each 10cm (4in) in diameter, using 300g/10oz ready-made or homemade puff pastry
- 2 bunches of fresh wild rocket
- 150g (5oz) feta cheese
- Salt and freshly ground black pepper
- 2 tsp oregano or thyme leaves, to garnish

Directions:

Place the cherry tomatoes on a baking tray, cut side facing up. Drizzle over 1 tablespoon of the olive oil, then sprinkle with the garlic and season with salt and pepper.

Bake in a preheated oven, 160°C (fan 140°C)/325°F/gas mark 3, for 25 minutes, or until the tomatoes are nice and soft but not mushy. Remove from the oven, then increase the oven temperature to 180°C (fan 160°C)/350°F/gas mark 4.

Meanwhile, caramelize the onions. Melt the butter in a saucepan with 1 tablespoon of the olive oil. Add the onions and cook gently over a very low heat for about 10–12 minutes, stirring continuously – this is a long process that will make the experience very special. When the onions are caramelized but not brown (they should be dark pink), stir in the balsamic vinegar.

Divide the onions between the cooked pastry cases, then put them into the oven to reheat for 6 minutes.

Serve the tarts piled high with the rocket. Place a few warm roasted tomatoes round the edge and crumble the feta cheese generously on top. Drizzle with the remaining olive oil and garnish with chopped oregano or thyme leaves.

22. Pineapple Tart

Pineapple and white chocolate tart with a chocolate shortbread pastry crust.

Makes: 4 servings

Prep: 20 mins

Cook: 20 mins

Ingredients:

For the chocolate shortbread pastry:

- 1 ¼ cups all-purpose flour
- 3/8 cup unsalted butter
- Generous 3/8 cup white sugar
- 2 egg yolks
- 1/4 tsp baking powder
- 7 tsp cocoa powder
- Vanilla powder
- Salt

For the filling:

- Generous 3/8 cup cream
- 2 tsp glucose syrup
- 7 oz. white chocolate
- 3 oz. pineapple jam

For the decoration:

- 9 oz. fresh pineapple slices
- Confectioners' (icing) sugar

Directions:

Prepare the shortbread pastry: Mix the softened butter with the sugar, stir in a pinch of salt and the egg. Add the flour, baking powder, cocoa and a pinch of vanilla powder, then knead briefly until you have a smooth, even paste.

Plastic wrap the dough and refrigerate for one hour. On a lightly floured surface, roll out 9 oz. of the shortbread pastry to a thickness of 1/8 in (3 mm).

Line a buttered, floured cake tin with the pastry. Spread with pineapple jam and bake at 350 °F (180 °C) for 18 to 20 minutes. Remove and cool, then remove the tart from the tin.

Chop the white chocolate and put it in a bowl. Boil the cream with the syrup and pour it over the chocolate. Mix well until you have smooth, velvety cream.

Leave to cool and pour into the tart shell until it is filled up to the brim. Garnish with fresh pineapple slices, which have been washed and dried. Sprinkle with confectioners' sugar before serving.

23. Chocolate Strawberry Tart

Strawberry and chocolate tart with a chocolate shortbread pastry crust.

Makes: 4 servings

Prep: 20 mins

Cook: 20 mins

Ingredients:

For the chocolate shortbread pastry:

- 1 ¼ cups all-purpose flour
- 3/8 cup unsalted butter
- Generous 3/8 cup white sugar
- 2 egg yolks
- 1/4 tsp baking powder
- 7 tsp cocoa powder
- Vanilla powder
- Salt

For the filling:

- Generous 3/8 cup cream
- 2 tsp glucose syrup
- 7 oz. dark chocolate
- 3 oz. strawberry jam

For the decoration:

- 9 oz. fresh strawberries
- Confectioners' (icing) sugar

Directions:

Prepare the shortbread pastry: Mix the softened butter with the sugar, stir in a pinch of salt and the egg. Add the flour, baking powder, cocoa and a pinch of vanilla powder, then knead briefly until you have a smooth, even paste.

Plastic wrap the dough and refrigerate for one hour. On a lightly floured surface, roll out 9 oz. of the shortbread pastry to a thickness of 1/8 in (3 mm).

Line a buttered, floured cake tin with the pastry. Spread with jam and bake at 350 °F (180 °C) for 18 to 20 minutes. Remove and cool, then remove the tart from the tin.

Chop the chocolate. Boil the cream with the syrup and pour it over the chocolate. Mix well until you have smooth, velvety cream.

Leave to cool and pour into the tart shell until it is filled up to the brim. Garnish with fresh strawberries, which have been washed and dried. Sprinkle with confectioners' sugar before serving.

24. Blackberry Tart

Blackberry and white chocolate tart with a chocolate shortbread pastry crust.

Makes: 4 servings

Prep: 20 mins

Cook: 20 mins

Ingredients:

For the chocolate shortbread pastry:

- 1 ¼ cups all-purpose flour
- 3/8 cup unsalted butter
- Generous 3/8 cup white sugar
- 2 egg yolks
- 1/4 tsp baking powder
- 7 tsp cocoa powder
- Vanilla powder
- Salt

For the filling:

- Generous 3/8 cup cream
- 2 tsp glucose syrup
- 7 oz. white chocolate
- 3 oz. blackberry jam

For the decoration:

- 9 oz. fresh blackberries
- Confectioners' (icing) sugar

Directions:

Prepare the shortbread pastry: Mix the softened butter with the sugar, stir in a pinch of salt and the egg. Add the flour, baking powder, cocoa and a pinch of vanilla powder, then knead briefly until you have a smooth, even paste.

Plastic wrap the dough and refrigerate for one hour. On a lightly floured surface, roll out 9 oz. of the shortbread pastry to a thickness of 1/8 in (3 mm).

Line a buttered, floured cake tin with the pastry. Spread with jam and bake at 350 °F (180 °C) for 18 to 20 minutes. Remove and cool, then remove the tart from the tin.

Chop the white chocolate & put it in a bowl. Boil the cream with the syrup and pour it over the chocolate. Mix well until you have smooth, velvety cream.

Leave to cool and pour into the tart shell until it is filled up to the brim. Garnish with fresh berries, which have been washed and dried. Sprinkle with confectioners' sugar before serving.

25. Peach Galette

This rustic dessert, with its golden crust and shiny, glazed peaches, makes a beautiful presentation at the table.

Makes: 6 servings

Prep: 1 hr. 10 mins

Cook: 40 mins

Ingredients:

Pastry

- ⅓ cup sour cream
- ½ cup ice-cold water
- 1½ cups all-purpose flour
- ⅓ cup yellow cornmeal
- 3 teaspoons sugar, plus 1 tablespoon for sprinkling on the prebaked dough
- ½ teaspoon salt
- 10 tablespoons chilled unsalted butter, cut into 8 pieces

Filling

- 20 peaches, halved and pitted
- ½ cup sugar
- 2 tablespoons cornstarch
- 2 teaspoons fresh lemon juice

Glaze

- 5 tablespoons peach jam or marmalade
- 3 tablespoons water

Directions:

To prepare the pastry, whisk together the sour cream and ice water in a small bowl. Set aside.

Place the flour, cornmeal, the 3 teaspoons sugar, and salt in a large bowl. Mix with a dry whisk or your fingers until well blended. Add the butter. Mix with your hands, a pastry blender, or in a food processor until the pieces of butter are pea-sized (8 to 10 pulses in the food processor). Add the sour cream mixture, 1 tablespoon at a time, gently mixing after each addition. Once all the liquid has been added, form the dough into a large disk. Don't handle the dough too much, and work quickly so that the butter stays cold. Wrap & refrigerate for 1 to 2 hours.

Mix the peaches in a bowl with the sugar, cornstarch, and lemon juice.

Preheat to 400°F.

To prepare the glaze, place the jam, water in a saucepan. Bring to a boil over med-low heat. Remove from the heat and set aside.

To prepare the galette, roll out the dough on a slightly floured surface until you have a 14- to 16"circle. Lightly flour the top of the dough. Fold dough over the pin & transfer to an 8-inch cast iron skillet. Gently press into the bottom and against the sides of the skillet. It just needs to stick to the sides while you add the filling. Arrange the peaches in the pan in a circular pattern, slightly overlapping one another, skin side up, starting at the outer edges and working toward the center. Quickly reheat the glaze and spoon over the peaches. Fold the edges over the fruit. It will form pleats, which is the result you want. You should have a roughly 2- to 3-inch border of dough folded in all around the edges. Sprinkle the peaches and crust with the 1 tablespoon sugar. Bake for 25 to 30 minutes. Serve in the skillet with vanilla ice cream or whipped cream.

26. Dark Chocolate Blackberry Tart

Blackberry and dark chocolate tart with a chocolate shortbread pastry crust.

Makes: 4 servings

Prep: 20 mins

Cook: 20 mins

Ingredients:

For the chocolate shortbread pastry:

- 1 ¼ cups all-purpose flour
- 3/8 cup unsalted butter
- Generous 3/8 cup white sugar
- 2 egg yolks
- 1/4 tsp baking powder
- 7 tsp cocoa powder
- Vanilla powder
- Salt

For the filling:

- Generous 3/8 cup cream
- 2 tsp glucose syrup
- 7 oz. dark chocolate
- 3 oz. blackberry jam

For the decoration:

- 9 oz. fresh blackberries
- Confectioners' (icing) sugar

Directions:

Prepare the shortbread pastry: Mix the softened butter with the sugar, stir in a pinch of salt and the egg. Add the flour, baking powder, cocoa and a pinch of vanilla powder, then knead briefly until you have a smooth, even paste.

Plastic wrap the dough and refrigerate for one hour. On a lightly floured surface, roll out 9 oz. of the shortbread pastry to a thickness of 1/8 in (3 mm).

Line a buttered, floured cake tin with the pastry. Spread with jam and bake at 350 °F (180 °C) for 18 to 20 minutes. Remove and cool, then remove the tart from the tin.

Chop the dark chocolate & put it in a bowl. Boil the cream with the syrup and pour it over the chocolate. Mix well until you have smooth, velvety cream.

Leave to cool and pour into the tart shell until it is filled up to the brim. Garnish with fresh berries, which have been washed and dried. Sprinkle with confectioners' sugar before serving.

27. Lime Tart

Sweet, zesty and light, this tart is the perfect after-dessert treat.

Makes: 8 servings

Prep: 2 hrs. 10 mins

Cook: 30 mins

Ingredients:

For the pastry:

- 1 ¾ cup all-purpose flour
- 4 tbsp. icing sugar
- ½ tsp salt
- ¼ cup unsweetened cocoa powder
- ½ cup unsalted butter
- 1 egg yolk
- 2 ½ tbsp. cold water

For the tart:

- ½ cup dark chocolate, grated finely
- 2 large limes
- 2/3 cup caster sugar
- 4 eggs
- ½ cup + 2 tbsp. heavy cream
- Icing sugar, for dusting

Directions:

For the pastry:

In a bowl, combine together the salt, cocoa, sugar, and flour. Add the butter and mix. Add the egg yolk and then the water. Mix well. Fold into a lump. Wrap with cling film and chill for 40 minutes.

Roll out the pastry evenly onto the base of a well-greased 9-inch spring form cake tin and chill for 90 minutes.

For the tart:

Preheat oven to 400°F. Place in the oven for 15 minutes. Do not overbake. Immediately sprinkle the hot pastry evenly with the grated chocolate. Set aside. Reduce oven temperature to 325°F.

Grate the zest into a bowl. Add the sugar and the juice from the limes. Mix well. Whisk in the eggs and then the cream until well incorporated. Pour over the pastry in the spring form tin and bake for about 30 minutes or until set.

Release the spring form-tin sides to aid cooling. Allow to cool completely. Dust with sugar and serve.

28. Strawberry and Basil Tart

Fresh and delicious strawberries and basil tart recipe.

Makes: 8 servings

Prep: 15 mins

Cook: 20 mins

Ingredients:

- 1 × plain sponge cake, 20cm (8in) in diameter
- 1 × blind-baked sweet short crust pastry case
- 5 tbsp strawberry jam
- 500g (1lb) strawberries

For the basil syrup

- 125ml (4fl oz) water
- 125g (4oz) golden caster sugar
- 6 basil leaves

Directions:

To make the basil syrup, put the water and sugar into a saucepan and heat to boiling point. Add the basil & leave to infuse for as long as possible – ideally overnight.

Preheat the oven to 400F. Cut the sponge cake in half, horizontally across the center.

Spread one 1/2 of the cake with strawberry jam and place it jam side down in the cooked pastry shell. Put the other 1/2 of the sponge cake to one side for another day.

Remove the basil leaves & discard them, then spoon the syrup over the sponge until it is evenly soaked.

Cover the tart with the strawberries and bake in the oven for 15 minutes or until the berries are hot and oozing juice. Serve immediately.

29. Dark Chocolate Orange Tart

Orange and dark chocolate tart with a chocolate shortbread pastry crust.

Makes: 4 servings

Prep: 20 mins

Cook: 20 mins

Ingredients:

For the chocolate shortbread pastry:

- 1 ¼ cups all-purpose flour
- 3/8 cup unsalted butter
- Generous 3/8 cup white sugar
- 2 egg yolks
- 1/4 tsp baking powder
- 7 tsp cocoa powder
- Vanilla powder
- Salt

For the filling:

- Generous 3/8 cup cream
- 2 tsp glucose syrup
- 7 oz. dark chocolate
- 3 oz. orange jam

For the decoration:

- 9 oz. fresh orange slices
- Confectioners' (icing) sugar

Directions:

Prepare the shortbread pastry: Mix the softened butter with the sugar, stir in a pinch of salt and the egg. Add the flour, baking powder, cocoa and a pinch of vanilla powder, then knead briefly until you have a smooth, even paste.

Plastic wrap the dough and refrigerate for one hour. On a lightly floured surface, roll out 9 oz. of the shortbread pastry to a thickness of 1/8 in (3 mm).

Line a buttered, floured cake tin with the pastry. Spread with jam and bake at 350 °F (180 °C) for 18 to 20 minutes. Remove and cool, then remove the tart from the tin.

Chop the dark chocolate & put it in a bowl. Boil the cream with the syrup and pour it over the chocolate. Mix well until you have smooth, velvety cream.

Leave to cool and pour into the tart shell until it is filled up to the brim. Garnish with fresh orange slices, which have been washed and dried. Sprinkle with confectioners' sugar before serving.

30. White Chocolate Apricot Tart

Apricot and white chocolate tart with a chocolate shortbread pastry crust.

Makes: 4 servings

Prep: 20 mins

Cook: 20 mins

Ingredients:

For the chocolate shortbread pastry:

- 1 ¼ cups all-purpose flour
- 3/8 cup unsalted butter
- Generous 3/8 cup white sugar
- 2 egg yolks
- 1/4 tsp baking powder
- 7 tsp cocoa powder
- Vanilla powder
- Salt

For the filling:

- Generous 3/8 cup cream
- 2 tsp glucose syrup
- 7 oz. white chocolate
- 3 oz. apricot jam

For the decoration:

- 9 oz. fresh apricot slices
- Confectioners' (icing) sugar

Directions:

Prepare the shortbread pastry: Mix the softened butter with the sugar, stir in a pinch of salt and the egg. Add the flour, baking powder, cocoa and a pinch of vanilla powder, then knead briefly until you have a smooth, even paste.

Plastic wrap the dough and refrigerate for one hour. On a lightly floured surface, roll out 9 oz. of the shortbread pastry to a thickness of 1/8 in (3 mm).

Line a buttered, floured cake tin with the pastry. Spread with jam and bake at 350 °F (180 °C) for 18 to 20 minutes. Remove and cool, then remove the tart from the tin.

Chop the white chocolate & put it in a bowl. Boil the cream with the syrup and pour it over the chocolate. Mix well until you have smooth, velvety cream.

Leave to cool and pour into the tart shell until it is filled up to the brim. Garnish with fresh apricot slices, which have been washed and dried. Sprinkle with confectioners' sugar before serving.

Conclusion

Well, there you go! 30 tart recipes for you to try out! Make sure you try out each recipe and don't forget to share with your friends and family! We hope you've enjoyed this book!

About the Author

A native of Indianapolis, Indiana, Valeria Ray found her passion for cooking while she was studying English Literature at Oakland City University. She decided to try a cooking course with her friends and the experience changed her forever. She enrolled at the Art Institute of Indiana which offered extensive courses in the culinary Arts. Once Ray dipped her toe in the cooking world, she never looked back.

When Valeria graduated, she worked in French restaurants in the Indianapolis area until she became the head chef at one of the 5-star establishments in the area. Valeria's attention to taste and visual detail caught the eye of a local business person who expressed an interest in publishing her recipes. Valeria began her secondary career authoring cookbooks and e-books which she tackled with as much talent and gusto as her first career. Her passion for food leaps off the page of her books which have colourful anecdotes and stunning pictures of dishes she has prepared herself.

Valeria Ray lives in Indianapolis with her husband of 15 years, Tom, her daughter, Isobel and their loveable Golden Retriever, Goldy. Valeria enjoys cooking special dishes in her large, comfortable kitchen where the family gets involved in preparing meals. This successful, dynamic chef is an inspiration to culinary students and novice cooks everywhere.

•••••••••• ● ● ● ● ●●•••••••

Author's Afterthoughts

Thank you for Purchasing my book and taking the time to read it from front to back. I am always grateful when a reader chooses my work and I hope you enjoyed it!

With the vast selection available online, I am touched that you chose to be purchasing my work and take valuable time out of your life to read it. My hope is that you feel you made the right decision.

I very much would like to know what you thought of the book. Please take the time to write an honest and informative review on Amazon.com. Your experience and opinions will be of great benefit to me and those readers looking to make an informed choice.

With much thanks,

Valeria Ray

Made in the USA
Monee, IL
11 November 2020